BUCKEYE

PEARL CRESCENT

SPRING AZURE

CABBAGE

TIGER SWALLOWTAIL

GREAT SPANGLED FRITILLARY

PURPLISH COPPER

LARGE WOOD NYMPH

QUEEN

COMMON
SOOTY WING

Can you name the butterflies inside the book? The endpapers will help you identify them. Left to right on the following pages: p. 4 (top), anise swallow-tail; p. 4 (bottom), spring azure, great spangled fritillary; p. 5 (top), queen; p. 5 (bottom), Baltimore, common sulphur, buckeye; p. 6, mourning cloak, large wood nymph; p. 7, silver-spotted skipper, spicebush swallowtail; p. 8, large wood nymph; p. 9, spicebush swallowtail; p. 10 (top), zebra swallowtail, anise swallowtail; p. 10 (bottom), mustard white, falcate orange tip, dog-face; p. 11 (top), purplish copper, bronze copper, silvery blue, gray hairstreak; p. 11 (bottom), question mark, painted lady, red-spotted purple; p. 12, silver-spotted skipper, common sooty wing, checkered skipper; p. 13, checkered skipper, silver-spotted skipper; p. 14, monarch, red admiral; p. 15 (top), tiger swallowtail, spring azure; p. 15 (bottom), common sulphur; p. 16, buckeye, viceroy, pearl crescent; p. 17 (top), Milbert's tortoise shell, giant swallow-tail; p. 17 (bottom), brown elfin, painted lady; p. 18, comma, red-spotted purple, viceroy; p. 19 (top), buckeye, common sulphur, tiger swallowtail; p. 19 (bottom), common sulphur, dogface, common sulphur; p. 20, alfalfa, columbine dusky wing, painted lady; p. 21, checkered white, Baltimore, eastern tailed blue; p. 22, eastern black swallowtail, cabbage; p. 24, eastern black swallowtails; p. 27, eastern black swallowtail; p. 28, eastern black swallowtail

Butterflies in the Garden
Copyright © 2002 by Carol Lerner
Manufactured in China. All rights reserved.
www.harperchildrens.com

Library of Congress Cataloging-in-Publication Data
Lerner, Carol.
Butterflies in the garden / Carol Lerner.
p.   cm.
ISBN 0-688-17478-7 — ISBN 0-688-17479-5 (lib. bdg.)
I. Butterfly gardening—Juvenile literature.   2. Butterflies—Juvenile literature.   [I. Butterflies.   2. Butterfly gardening.]
I. Title.
QL544.6 .L47   2002   595.78'9—dc21   00-061408   CIP   AC

Typography by Stephanie Bart-Horvath
7 8 9 10
❖
First Edition

Butterflies in the Garden

CAROL LERNER

HarperCollins*Publishers*

CALENDULA   RED VALERIAN

It is a bright summer day, and butterflies have come to
the garden. Their wings flash in the sunlight as they hover over
the flowers.

   Some butterflies flutter above the plants for a moment and then
fly away.

6

BERGAMOT   GLOBE THISTLE   CORNFLOWER   DAY LILY

Others stay, landing on one flower after another. They press
their heads deep into the heart of each blossom and then <u>move</u> on
to the next flower.

What are they doing there?

DAY LILY FLOWER, CUT OPEN

NECTAR IS AT THE BOTTOM OF THE PETALS.

NECTAR IS INSIDE THIS TUBE.

A SINGLE VALERIAN FLOWER, CUT OPEN AND ENLARGED

They are looking for nectar.

Nectar is a sugary liquid that is made by some plants and stored deep within their flowers. It is the main food of most butterflies.

Some kinds of butterflies take nectar wherever they find it. Others eat from only certain kinds of flowers.

FEELERS

EYE

BUTTERFLY HEAD, WITH
PROBOSCIS UNROLLED

WITH PROBOSCIS
ROLLED

First the butterfly "tastes" the flower by touching it with special
hairs on the ends of its legs. When it finds nectar, a long tube, called
a proboscis (pro-BAHS-kiss), unrolls to reach the nectar supply.
After the butterfly has eaten, the proboscis rolls up into a tight coil.

There are so many different kinds of butterflies!

They are divided into groups called *families*. Their shapes and colors give us hints about what family each belongs to. Here are some you might see in your garden.

Swallowtails are large butterflies. They are named for the "tails" on their back wings. The tails look a little like the long forked tails of barn swallows.

Whites and sulphurs are small to medium with white, yellow, or orange wings.

Gossamer wings are small and colorful. Many are bright blue, red, or orange. This family includes the hairstreaks—butterflies with threadlike tails on their back wings, similar to the swallowtails'.

Brushfoots have many members in their family. Other butterflies walk on six legs, but brushfoots use only four. Their two front legs are very small and are covered with hair, like a brush. These legs are folded against their bodies. Some brushfoots have dull colors, but many are bright and boldly marked.

COSMOS

NASTURTIUM

Skippers are small to medium in size. Most have orange or brown coloring. Skippers are known for their thick bodies and little hooks at the ends of their feelers. They are quick and darting.

MARIGOLD

ZINNIA

Invite butterflies to your own yard by planting flowers with plenty of nectar. Arrange the flowers in groups, with three or more of the same kind growing close together. A big splash of color will get the attention of hungry butterflies.

These butterfly plants grow quickly. You can plant seeds in spring and have flowers by summer.

NICOTIANA

PETUNIA

Or you can buy plants with some of the butterflies' favorite
flowers from a garden center.

SWEET WILLIAM   *HELIOTROPE*   *JOHNNY-JUMP-UP*   *SNAPDRAGON*

Transplant them to a sunny spot in your garden.

PURPLE CONEFLOWER

PHLOX

DAISY

ASTER

Instead of using flowers that will live for just one summer, you can buy some perennial butterfly plants. They will come back year after year to bloom in your garden.

16

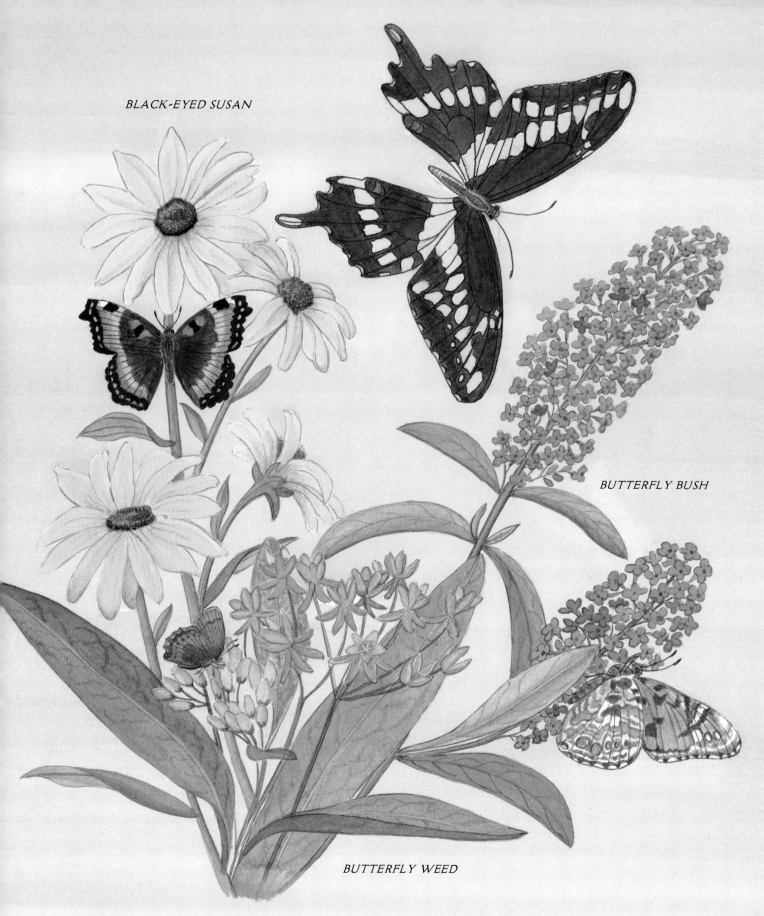

BLACK-EYED SUSAN

BUTTERFLY BUSH

BUTTERFLY WEED

Never use poisons on any of the plants in your garden. Poisons that kill plant pests will hurt the butterflies too.

17

There are other ways to lure butterflies to your yard. Some like the taste of rotting fruit! Mash up a banana or some soft overripe fruit with a little sugar or honey. Put it out in the sun next to your flower garden and watch for visitors.

And some butterflies flock to wet spots on the ground to sip water from the earth. Butterfly watchers call this *puddling*. Make a puddle by placing a shallow pan or plate on the ground. Fill it to the brim with sand or mud and keep it wet. Add a few stones for the butterflies to sit on.

LUPINE

COLUMBINE

HOLLYHOCK

You will see some butterflies moving from plant to plant without feeding. These are females looking for places to leave eggs. Each kind of butterfly searches for its own special kind of plant—one that will feed the young caterpillars when they hatch from the eggs.

CLEOME

TURTLEHEAD

FALSE INDIGO

If you have the right plants for their caterpillars to eat,
butterflies may lay their eggs in your yard.

Some butterflies look for these garden favorites.

21

Other kinds of butterflies lay their eggs on the leaves of vegetables that you can grow in your garden.

PARSLEY

CABBAGE

CARROT

Some common weedy plants are food for many kinds of caterpillars. Do you have a sunny corner where you could let long grasses and weeds grow for a summer?

WHITE SWEET CLOVER

THISTLE

MILKWEED

PINK CLOVER

23

QUEEN ANNE'S LACE

THE EGG IS ABOUT THE SIZE OF THE HEAD OF A PIN.

Keep your eyes on these plants on sunny days when butterflies are flying. Look over the leaves and stems after butterflies visit and try to find these tiny eggs. You might be able to watch as the eggs hatch and the caterpillars grow.

When it is old enough to leave its egg, the caterpillar wriggles out. The tiny caterpillar is an eating machine, with strong jaws for chewing the plant. It eats and grows until it is too big for its skin.

Then the skin splits apart, and the caterpillar crawls out in a fresh new skin. And goes on eating until it must shed its skin again . . .

and again . . .   and again . . .

and again!

Finally the full-grown caterpillar stops eating. It moves to a safe resting place on a plant and attaches itself there.

Its skin splits for the last time, leaving the caterpillar hanging from the plant, covered by a hard, thin shell. It stays there for days or weeks, not moving. But inside its tough shell great changes are going on. The caterpillar is becoming a butterfly.

At last the shell splits open and the new butterfly crawls out.

It waits until its crumpled wings
spread out to their full size. Then the
butterfly lifts off on its first flight . . .

and sails through the air in search of nectar flowers.

Good luck with your butterfly garden!

QUESTION MARK

BROWN ELFIN

FALCATE
ORANGE TIP

ZEBRA SWALLOWTAIL

MILBERT'S TORTOISE SHELL

GIANT SWALLOWTAIL

EASTERN BLACK
SWALLOWTAIL

EASTERN
TAILED BLUE

COMMA